Materials

Glass

Cassie Mayer

Heinemann Library
Chicago, Illinois

Customer Service 888-454-2279
Visit our website at www.heinemannraintree.com

Picture research: Tracy Cummins and Heather Mauldin
Designed by Joanna Hinton-Malivoire
Printed in China by South China Printing Company Limited

12 11 10 09 08
10 9 8 7 6 5 4 3 2 1

ISBN-13: 978-1-4329-1620-6 (hc)
ISBN-13: 978-1-4329-1629-9 (pb)

The Library of Congress has cataloged the first edition as follows:
Mayer, Cassie.
  Glass / Cassie Mayer.
    p. cm. -- (Materials)
  Includes bibliographical references and index.
  ISBN 978-1-4329-1620-6 (hc) -- ISBN 978-1-4329-1629-9 (pb) 1. Glass--Juvenile literature. I. Title.
  TP857.3.M39 2008
  620.1'44--dc22
                                2008005580

Acknowledgments
The author and publisher are grateful to the following for permission to reproduce copyright material: ©Age Fotostock pp. **4** (Targa), **15** (Dinodia); ©Alamy p. **5** (Peter Arnold, Inc./ Oldrich Karasek); ©Corbis pp. **11**, **23T** (Keystone/ Martin Reutschi); ©drr.net p. **13** (Kenneth M. Jones); ©Getty Images p. **12** (Yuka Kisugi); ©Heinemann Raintree pp. **7**, **8**, **9**, **14**, **17**, **18**, **19**, **21**, **22ALL**, **23B** (David Rigg); ©istockphoto p. **20** (Maciej Korzekwa); ©Shutterstock pp. **6** (Jo Ann Snover), **10** (Semjonow Juri), **16** (David Scheuber).

Cover image used with permission of ©agefotostock (Sylvain Grandadam). Back cover image used with permission of ©Heinemann Raintree (David Rigg).

Every effort has been made to contact copyright holders of any material reproduced in this book. Any omissions will be rectified in subsequent printings if notice is given to the publisher.

Contents

What Is Glass? 4

What Happens When Glass
   Is Heated?. 10

Recycling Glass 14

How Do We Use Glass?. 18

Things Made of Glass 22

Picture Glossary. 23

Content Vocabulary for Teachers . 23

Note to Parents and Teachers 24

What Is Glass?

Glass is made from sand.

Glass is made by people.

Glass can be clear.

Glass can be colored.

Glass can break.

Glass cannot bend.

What Happens When Glass Is Heated?

Glass can get hot.

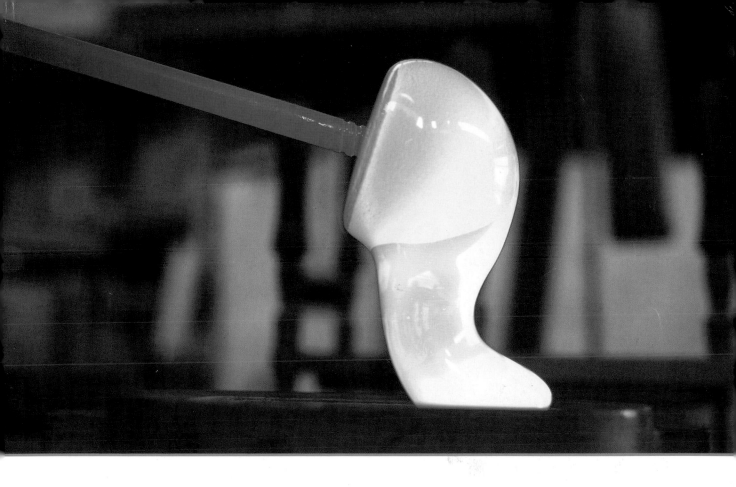

Glass can melt.

Glass can become cool in the air.

Glass can become a new shape.

Recycling Glass

Glass can be recycled.

Glass can be used to make new glass.

Glass can be used to make
new bottles.

Glass can be used to make new glasses.

How Do We Use Glass?

Glass can be used to make windows.

Glass can be used to make dishes.

Glass can be used to make light bulbs.

Glass can be used to make many things.

Things Made of Glass

◀ drinking glasses

vases ▶

Picture Glossary

melt to change from a solid into a liquid. Some materials melt when heated.

recycle to take old things and break them down. Then they are made into new things.

Content Vocabulary for Teachers

material Something that takes up space and can be used to make other things

Index

bend, 9

break, 8

color, 7

clear, 6

sand, 4

recycle, 14

light bulb, 20

Note to Parents and Teachers

Before reading

Ask children to make a list of objects that are made from glass. Can they think of glass objects that are clear, or colored, or opaque? Help children find a few glass objects indoors. Ask them to describe how the objects feel and look.

After reading

• Turn to pages 4-5, and 10-14 and ask children to reflect on how glass is made. Ask them to guess how glass is colored.

• Ask children to collect recyclable glass objects for a week. Then, at the end of the week, take the children to a recycling center so that they can return their glass objects to be recycled.